Treasure in the Trees

Written by
Christopher Cheng

Illustrated by
Erika Meza

ISBN-13: 978-0-328-83286-6
ISBN-10: 0-328-83286-3
5 6 7 8 9 10 V0B4 19 18 17 16

Contents

Chapter 1
The Secret

Nisha stood under the shelter of her tree, deep in the backyard, and looked up. She had a secret in her tree, but nobody believed the truth . . . except maybe her dog Scruggs!

Nisha sat down beside the gnarled tree trunk—she had a decision to make. Should she go ahead with her plan, to try to tell her parents the secret again, and risk their scowls of disbelief? Or just give up?

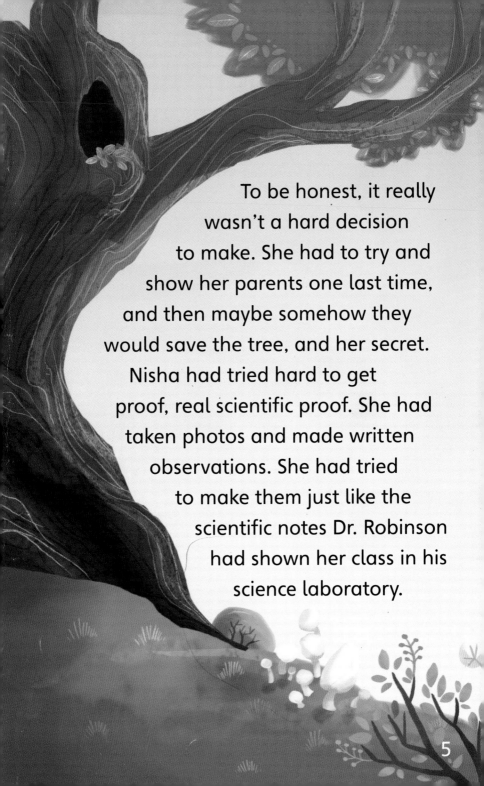

To be honest, it really wasn't a hard decision to make. She had to try and show her parents one last time, and then maybe somehow they would save the tree, and her secret. Nisha had tried hard to get proof, real scientific proof. She had taken photos and made written observations. She had tried to make them just like the scientific notes Dr. Robinson had shown her class in his science laboratory.

Then again, Nisha's parents knew that she was really good at manipulating images on the computer. She had even once placed her grandparents' heads on the bodies of two giant tortoises! Nisha thought it was hilarious, but her parents had banned her from using the computer for a week, except for school work.

   This time she
would have to convince
her mom and dad that her
proof was real. Not only would she have
to present her scientific evidence, but she
would also have to *show* them her secret.
She remembered what Dr. Robinson had
said to the class: "Science can reveal the
truth. But until people see with their own
two eyes, they won't believe."

The next problem was getting her parents' attention. Before they had opened the shop, Nisha's parents always had time for her. Now they were hardly ever at home.

"We might have bitten off more than we can chew," Nisha sometimes heard her father say when he got home after a long day at the shop. Her mother always replied, "It will all be fine . . . if we can survive until the end of the month." The months were going by though, and things weren't getting better.

Nisha's dad used to love cooking meals for them, but now they had frozen dinners instead. He was always too tired to cook. Nisha's mom never had any time to go shopping with her. Nisha didn't like shopping now anyway. Thankfully, she still had her trusty spaniel, Scruggs, and of course, her secret.

But tonight Nisha would be sharing her secret, and not just with her mom and dad. The property developer would be back later. When he first came to the door in September, Nisha's parents had thought he was the answer to all their problems. That was when Nisha's problems *really* started.

Chapter 2
A Strange Discovery

It had all begun with lots of dog barking.

"Nisha, please go and stop Scruggs from barking," said Dad, exasperated. Her parents had bought the dog to keep her company, and she loved him, but he consumed so much of her time.

"Have you taken the dog for a walk? Did you feed him his dinner? Clean up that mess he left on the lawn!" Her parents' voices echoed in her ears. "*Now* please, Nisha!" Before the shop, she had never needed a dog to keep her company, but now that her parents worked non-stop, she figured a dog was better than an empty house.

Nisha followed the sound of the barks to find Scruggs. It was coming from outside. She walked down to the grove of trees at the back of their house and pushed her way inside. She loved the grove. It was her own forest, her special place. She loved coming in here at all times of the day to sit and sing, to watch the trees, and to weave daisy chains in the summer. Sometimes she even thought she could hear the trees sing.

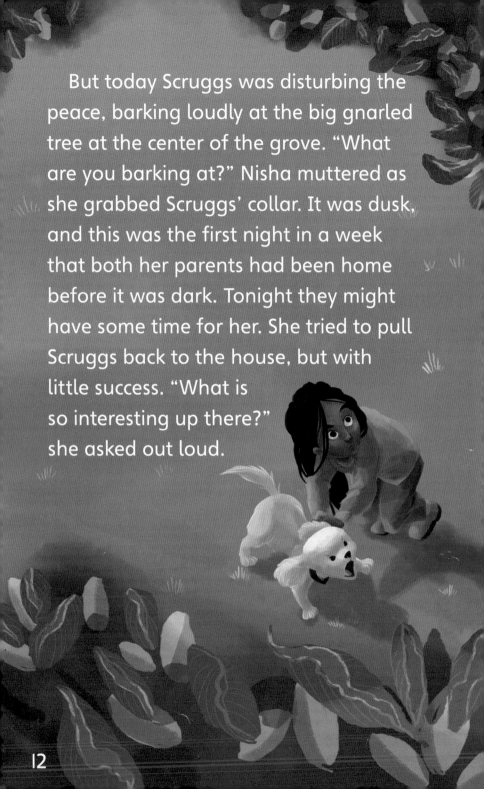

But today Scruggs was disturbing the peace, barking loudly at the big gnarled tree at the center of the grove. "What are you barking at?" Nisha muttered as she grabbed Scruggs' collar. It was dusk, and this was the first night in a week that both her parents had been home before it was dark. Tonight they might have some time for her. She tried to pull Scruggs back to the house, but with little success. "What is so interesting up there?" she asked out loud.

Nisha followed Scruggs' stare up the tree trunk, along the branches to the leaves. She could see nothing.

She started to get frustrated and pulled at Scruggs' collar, but then, suddenly, she saw a strange shining pattern catch the last rays of sunlight on the underside of one leaf.

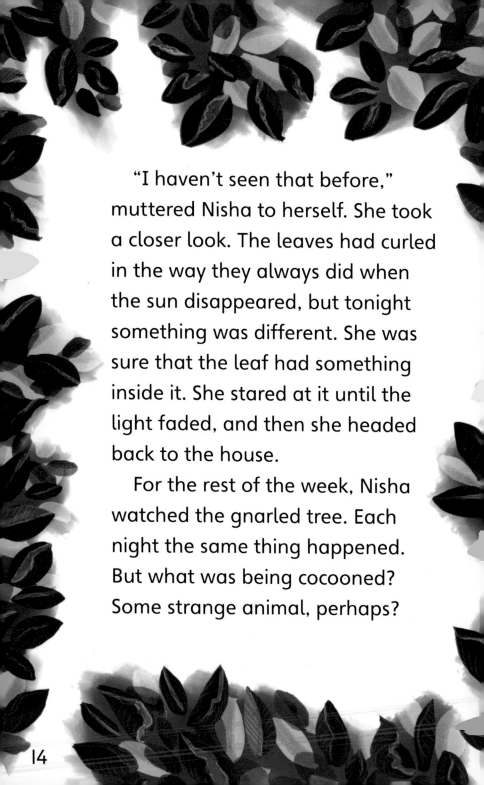

"I haven't seen that before," muttered Nisha to herself. She took a closer look. The leaves had curled in the way they always did when the sun disappeared, but tonight something was different. She was sure that the leaf had something inside it. She stared at it until the light faded, and then she headed back to the house.

For the rest of the week, Nisha watched the gnarled tree. Each night the same thing happened. But what was being cocooned? Some strange animal, perhaps?

Chapter 3
The Grove

On Thursday evening they all sat down for dinner as usual, but Nisha thought something felt different. Her parents were acting strangely. It took a while for her to realize that it was because they looked happier. Dad said he wanted to talk to her about something to do with the trees at the back of their house.

"Someone came by today to talk to me about the grove," he said. "He was a property developer. His company is interested in buying the grove for land to build houses . . . you know we could really use that money."

Her mom smiled. "It's the miracle we've been hoping for!"

"Come, this way," urged Nisha as she led her parents down to the grove later that evening. Even though she was sure she was doing the right thing, she was nervous about sharing what she had seen with them.

"What are you doing, Nisha? I was washing the dishes and I still have work to do," Dad sighed as he followed her.

"Come and see," she said as she hurried them toward the grove. "Look. Up there," she said, pointing to the leaves.

"There's nothing there, Nisha," said Dad. "It's just leaves and branches. Let's just go back to the house now."

"But it *is* there. I saw it. Something is wrapped inside those leaves," Nisha protested. "What if it's important? What if it's a new species, or a rare creature?"

"There is nothing there," said Mom, frustrated.

"And besides . . ." Now it was her father with a not-so-happy look on his face. "The leaves are too high up to see clearly. Maybe it was just the light playing tricks on your eyes."

"But there is something there," sighed Nisha. "I know I saw it."

"The leaves are the same as always. They open in the day. They curl up at night to conserve energy." Her father gave a steely look that meant this conversation was over.

Nisha's heart sank.
There was something
in that tree, something
special, and she wasn't
about to let it be
destroyed. Now
she knew what
she had to do.
She needed proof.

Chapter 4
Proof

If her parents needed proof, then Nisha would get it. Finally she could put into practice the skills she had learned in science class with Dr. Robinson.

Early on Saturday morning she collected her notebook and pencils, and with determined steps she marched down to the tree. Scruggs followed her excitedly, his tail wagging behind him as he ran.

Nisha sat down beneath the tree with its arching branches and dense foliage and flipped open her notebook. "This is *real* science," she thought.

She carefully wrote the date and time in her book, just as Dr. Robinson had taught Nisha's class. She remembered his instructions about careful, accurate, close observations. He warned not to use your imagination. "Write what you see and not what you think you know. Record the things that you can observe," he always stated.

So then Nisha began recording her observations:

Saturday, September 15, 9:16 a.

- Rough trunk, gnarled near the base

- Small hole, the size of a human head, in trunk near branch, might be nesting hole

- Gray and brown bark

- Unfurled (nice word!) leaves

- Leaves: red underside, look green on top

- Sounds: all quiet, except for the wind whispering through the leaves

She was sure about all of it, except the leaves. That part she wasn't 100 percent sure about because from underneath she couldn't see what the tops of the leaves looked like. Remembering what Dr. Robinson had said, she hastily added a question mark.

And then she heard it. A low rumbling sound. It wasn't coming from the tree. It was her stomach! The morning had passed in a flash. Her stomach rumbled again even louder. She was thirsty too. She knew that in the laboratory *No Food or Drink* signs were stuck everywhere. But Dr. Robinson had also said, "In the field, scientists need to be prepared for long periods of observation."

Nisha knew she couldn't spend all day without food and water. She desperately wanted to keep observing, but when her stomach rumbled again she knew she needed FOOD! Nisha left her pencils with her notebook at the base of the tree and ran back to the house. She hadn't been gone for more than ten minutes, before she was back with her lunch next to her notebook and pencils—and a line of small, bright yellow blobs!

They started as a pile on her notebook and then became a trail that meandered around the tree, behind some bushes to an opening in the trunk. The opening looked like a large gnawed hole, and the yellow blobs led inside!

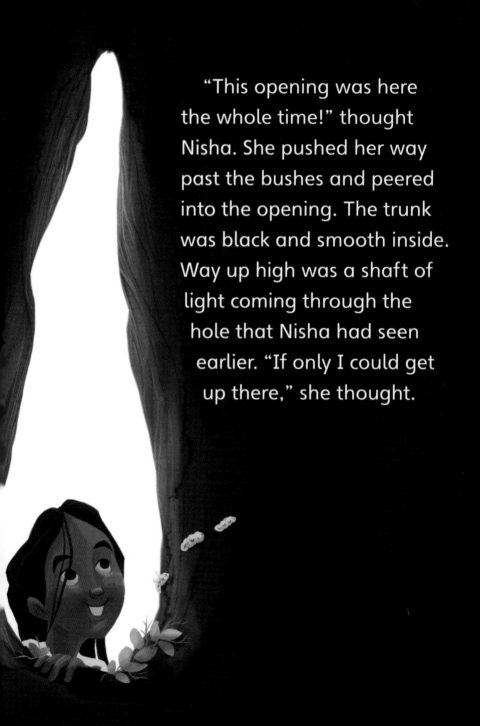

"This opening was here the whole time!" thought Nisha. She pushed her way past the bushes and peered into the opening. The trunk was black and smooth inside. Way up high was a shaft of light coming through the hole that Nisha had seen earlier. "If only I could get up there," she thought.

Chapter 5

More Observations

Forgetting her still-rumbling stomach, Nisha inched her way up inside the tree trunk. She used her strong arms and legs to climb hand over hand, foot over foot, until her head was at the opening. She saw the bright yellow blobs continue along the branch and onto the stems of each leaf.

Finally, a breakthrough! Nisha clambered back down the inside of the tree. She nibbled her lunch while recording her latest observations, adding sketches and labeling diagrams as she went.

It was late afternoon when she saw them again—the blobs were inching their way along the branches. "Oh, they are ugly!" exclaimed Nisha. Then she remembered Dr. Robinson saying, "Record the things that you can observe."

"If only I had my camera with me," she sighed as she drew the caterpillar-like creature on her page. She labeled the parts, especially the four big, long horns protruding from the body segments. She was just comparing the creatures to her sketch when she saw one of the creatures lift its back legs and leave a little yellow blob.

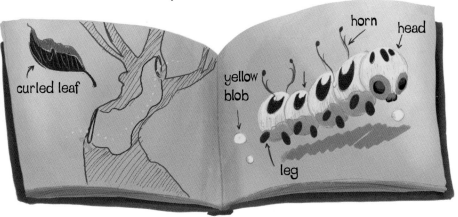

curled leaf

yellow blob

horn   head

leg

"Oh, yuck! Just as well I didn't sniff or taste that!" she thought. Then she remembered Dr. Robinson's words: "Collect samples." Next time she would have to bring a sample bag.

She continued watching the creature. It inched along the branch and the leaf stem and onto the leaf. Then, as the sun faded, the leaf curled and wrapped the creature like a bug in a rug.

"So that's what I saw!" she shouted out loud.

She had proof that these strange creatures existed! There was no way her parents would sell the grove to the developers now. When they came home from the shop, Nisha showed her parents the notebook.

"You have such an active imagination, dear Nisha!" said her mom, giggling. It was clear they didn't believe her.

"But—" started Nisha. Her dad cut her off. "Now wash up and let's all eat. We all need to talk about the trees and our decision. The developers made a very generous offer today. They'll be bringing us the paperwork tomorrow evening."

Nisha knew that she needed even more proof, and fast—because *her* grove with *her* tree was about to be sold to the developers and destroyed!

Nisha went straight back to the grove with her camera. She took photographs of the trunk, inside and out. She took photographs of the leaf litter and the leaves. Nisha focused on the curled leaves and kept on clicking and clicking.

She marched into the house, stepped over a sleeping Scruggs, and went straight to her computer. She uploaded the photos.

"Now I'll have the proof they need," Nisha said triumphantly.

But she didn't. The photos were blurry. She hadn't accounted for the fading light. It was too late now to take more. She would have to wait for tomorrow morning. But she also had another plan up her sleeve. She opened her e-mail and starting typing: *Dear Dr. Robinson* . . .

Chapter 6
Saved!

The next evening, Nisha was nervous.
The photos she'd taken that morning
had turned out perfectly, but she was still
worried that her parents would not believe
her. She geared up to show them . . . but
then there was a knock at the front door.

"That'll be the developer," said Dad.
"Answer the door please, Nisha." She
rushed and opened the door, hoping that
her plan had worked.

"Good evening, Nisha." It was Dr. Robinson. "Can I introduce you to my friend Professor Watkins? She works at the university in the Entomology Department, and she is so eager to meet you. We were fascinated by your e-mail about the creatures you've discovered. I'm sorry we couldn't make it here to witness the curling leaves in time."

"Tomorrow maybe," replied Nisha. "Why don't you come and meet my parents?"

She led the guests into the dining room and introduced them to her parents. Nisha's parents exchanged a puzzled look, but, seeing their daughter's excitement, they stood quietly while Nisha began her presentation on the creatures.

The professor examined the photos and the bright yellow sample that Nisha had collected. The professor and Dr. Robinson nodded in unison. Professor Watkins pored over Nisha's notebook and beamed. "I wish some of my students were as accurate as you." Nisha's parents' eyes opened wide.

After some time, a lot of explanation, and many cups of tea, everyone agreed. Nisha had indeed found something amazing, possibly even a new species!

"I always knew you were clever, but this? You're a real scientist! I'm sorry we didn't believe you," said Nisha's dad. "We were just so busy with the shop. I mean, we can't sell the grove now!"

He was interrupted by another knock at the door.

"Oh!" exclaimed Nisha's mother. "That'll be the developer." She cautiously opened the door and invited the developer in. Nisha's mom and dad took him into the living room and closed the door, leaving Nisha and the scientists in the dining room.

After what felt like forever, the developer left.

"What now?" Nisha asked her mom.

"Well, we've told him we absolutely can't sell now . . . but that still leaves us with a money problem."

"Oh, I wouldn't worry about that," said Professor Watkins. "That's probably the least of your worries. With what we have seen, we will apply for this area to be specially protected. I am sure you will receive compensation for that protection."

The family breathed a huge sigh of relief. Nisha's mom and dad embraced her in a huge hug.

"To our scientist, and her discovery!"

"Three cheers! Hip hip . . . "

"...**HOORAY!**"

Nisha smiled to herself. Science had won out in the end.